SHREDGUITAR
IMPROVISATION

The Creative Guide to Rock & Shred Metal Guitar Improvisation

CHRIS**ZOUPA**

FUNDAMENTAL**CHANGES**

Shred Guitar Improvisation

The Creative Guide to Rock & Shred Metal Guitar Improvisation

ISBN: 978-1-78933-087-8

Published by **www.fundamental-changes.com**

Copyright © 2019 Chris Zoupa

Edited by Tim Pettingale

The moral right of this author has been asserted.

www.fundamental-changes.com

Twitter: @guitar_joseph

Over 10,000 fans on Facebook: **FundamentalChangesInGuitar**

Instagram: **FundamentalChanges**

For over 350 Free Guitar Lessons with Videos Check Out

www.fundamental-changes.com

Cover Image Copyright: Chris Zoupa used by permission

Contents

Introduction

You might have had that dream where you're standing at the front of a classroom. You're making a speech, or maybe doing a "show and tell" of your favourite toy or comic book. Suddenly, you become aware that you are, in fact, naked and everyone in the class is laughing at you.

I still regularly have dreams like this, despite being 32 and having not entered a classroom for nearly 14 years. I'm hoping to use the proceeds of this book to get extensive therapy regarding why these dreams keep happening!

Many guitarists feel "naked" or put on the spot when called upon to spontaneously improvise a solo and experiences the same classroom terror described above. Here are some things I've heard guitarists say out loud hundreds of times:

"What if I screw up?"

"What if I lose my place?"

"Isn't it easier if I just write something."

If this sounds like you, you're in the right place. In this book I'm going to show you that improvisation can be super fun. It's just a matter of doing the preparation beforehand.

One of the biggest perceived obstacles guitarists have is knowing enough theory and having an awareness of how chords work. I know, yawn-fest! But doing some work on this aspect of playing is the launchpad from which magical, spur of the moment creativity and uninhibited stream of consciousness playing can take off!

In this book I'll show you how to play over chords, target certain chord tones to outline the changes, create memorable phrases without resorting to clichés, make scales sound less linear, and add general flair and pizazz to your playing.

Are you pumped? You should be!

Let's dive into the deep end together. Don't worry, I'll be with you whole time.

As Bud, the wise golden retriever once taught me, "Believe in yourself. The magic has been in you all along" – and he played Basketball and Soccer … with *humans*! Amazing right?!

Have fun!

Zoups

Get the Audio

The audio files for this book are available to download for free from **www.fundamental-changes.com.** The link is in the top right-hand corner. Simply select this book title from the drop-down menu and follow the instructions to get the audio.

We recommend that you download the files directly to your computer, not to your tablet, and extract them there before adding them to your media library. You can then put them on your tablet, iPod or burn them to CD. On the download page there is a help PDF and we also provide technical support via the contact form.

For over 350 Free Guitar Lessons with Videos Check out:

www.fundamental-changes.com

Over 10,000 fans on Facebook: **FundamentalChangesInGuitar**

Tag us for a share on Instagram: **FundamentalChanges**

Chapter 1 – Chord Tones and Chord Numbers

"But, Chris…!" I hear you cry, confronted with a diagram at the beginning of Chapter One, "…where are all the sexy licks?"

We'll get to that very soon. Mindless atonal shred can be fun and is an excellent way to annoy your loved ones and neighbours, but in order to make great music there are some basic principles you need to know.

A bit of Roman history

A basic understanding of major scale harmony goes a long way when it comes to improvising over a set of chord changes. If you know all this stuff inside out, feel free to skip ahead to the licks – but a theory refresher never hurt anyone.

Let's take the C Major scale for example. The scale is made up of the notes C D E F G A and B. Taking the first note of the scale, skipping the next one, and the one after that gives us our first three-note chord, called a triad: C E G it spells a basic C Major chord.

If we move to the second note in the scale (D) and repeat the process, we get D F A which spells a basic D minor chord. This is called harmonising the scale – in other words, turning it into chords.

Each chord in the harmonised scale is assigned a Roman numeral for shorthand. C Major is the I chord. D minor is the ii chord, and so on. (Major and dominant chords have upper case numbers and minor chords have lower case numbers – blame history!)

The table shows all the chords in the key of C Major. The Roman numeral system comes in handy later when you want to explain a chord progression to someone and make it understandable regardless of what key it will be played in. For example, your basic three-chord blues in C Major is a I IV V progression (C Major, F Major, G Major).

Roman Numeral shorthand	Chord Name
I	C Major
ii	D minor
iii	E minor
IV	F Major
V	G Major
vi	A minor
vii	B minor

Example 1a shows a very common classic rock chord progression (if you use your imagination, it sounds not unlike *Since You've Been Gone* by Rainbow).

The chords are C Major – G Major – A minor – F Major. The sequence in Roman numerals is I V vi IV.

Example 1a:

Now look at the triads that created these chords. The notes contained in each is as follows:

C Major = C E G

G Major = G B D

A minor = A C E

F Major = F A C

A triad contains the note intervals that are most important in identifying its flavour:

- The *root* note of the chord (C in the C Major chord)

- The *third* (E in C Major)

- The *fifth* (G in C Major)

Note: the third interval is a *major third* for major chords or a *minor third* for minor chords. "Minor third" just means the note is lowered a half step.

Why am I telling you this?

Well, if you want to play a super strong *articulate* solo when confronted with a set of chord changes, and you're unsure what to play, your first port of call is to *target* those strong notes that outline the chord changes. Once you become adept at this process, you can use tons of other creative ideas in between those chord tones, and your ideas will still sound strong and well defined.

Let me show you how it works in practice…

Targeting the root

Targeting the root note is as simple as playing the C note when a C Major chord is being played.

You might think, "But that's boring… *and* that's the bass player's job!" and there's a degree of truth to this. In a moment we'll be targeting the third and the fifth, but it's important to know where your root is at all times!

Let's get playing and begin simple. Don't worry, simple is good. If you're concerned the material here is beneath you, skip forward to the last chapter and see what you're letting yourself in for!

Begin by learning where the root notes are on each chord of the previous example: C, G, A and F.

Example 1b:

In a moment I'll show you a melodic lick that strongly follows these chord changes by targeting the root notes above. To do this I'll use two scales that sound great played over a chord progression in the key of C Major, and which fall easily on the guitar neck.

The A Minor Pentatonic and A Aeolian scales are built from the sixth note of the C Major scale. Play both scales over backing track one.

Example 1c:

Example 1d targets the root notes of each chord using licks built from the two scales above. The strong scale choice, combined with triad note targeting creates a significant emphasis on chord changes, as well as filling out the bars with interesting hooks and melodies.

Example 1d:

Focusing on the root like this creates a strong foundation for your melodic ideas. Players who have little awareness of the chord changes tend to have a "meandering" sound to their solos and don't often play memorable lines. Targeting the root and other triad notes will help keep your listeners engaged.

Targeting the 3rd

Next, we'll target the third interval of each chord in our progression. Once again, this might seem like a boring bassline to begin with, but the more you practice this the more the sound of each interval will become embedded, and you'll find yourself playing stronger melodic ideas.

The third interval emphasises the *emotional* major or minor quality of each chord and its happy or sad feeling. Notice how targeting the third sounds less "resolved" than targeting the root.

Example 1e:

Example 1f targets the thirds on the chord changes and fills out the bars with notes from the A Minor Pentatonic and A Aeolian scale shape to outline the sequence while building a meaningful solo.

Example 1f:

Targeting the 5th

Finally, let's learn to target the fifth interval of each chord.

On their own, these notes form a dull, uninspiring melody, but they do sound *stable*.

Example 1g:

Example 1h uses the A Minor Pentatonic and Aeolian scales again, while targeting the fifths.

Example 1h:

Targeting all three notes of the triad

Once you've practised targeting root, third and fifth separately, it's time to mix things up and target all three triad notes. You can be as organised as you like when practicing this technique, but we have to start somewhere so let's begin by targeting the following chord tones:

Over C Major we'll target the root (C)

Over G Major we'll target the major 3rd (B)

Over A minor we'll target the 5th (E)

Over F Major we'll target the major 3rd again (A)

Here is how that sounds:

Example 1i:

Example 1j combines these target notes with the A Minor Pentatonic and A Aeolian scales. You'll hear different the *colours* of each chord being highlighted.

Example 1j:

Now we've worked on targeting any triad note in each chord in the progression, practise this technique as follows:

1. Go back to the beginning and play through the progression using only root notes.

2. Compose a melodic line of your own that contains the root note of each chord falling on beat 1 when that chord is played in the backing track.

3. Now play through the progression highlighting only the third of each chord.

4. Compose a melodic line that highlights the third on each chord change.

5. Play through the progression highlighting only the fifth.

6. Compose a line highlighting the fifth on each change.

7. Finally, choose a target note "route" through the changes (i.e. third of C Major, root of G Major, fifth of A minor, root of F Major) and compose a melodic line that fits around it.

It's important to say at this point that a small percentage of improvisation occurs due to a happy accident. The more preparation you've done, the more likely it is that a beautiful line will come out of you by "accident". So, it's fine to write lines and build your vocabulary until you can play without really thinking about it.

In the initial stages, the things you play may sound stale and robotic, but rest assured that after enough experimentation you'll begin to find the phrasing and embellishments that bring out *your* voice as a musician. This is a journey of self-discovery. Yes, I'm aware that I sound like a pretentious douchebag writing a self-help book, but trust me, there's nothing less authentic than a mediocre regurgitation of stolen licks from your favourite players. We've all seen *that* guy at the guitar store, playing the same two SRV licks over and over. Never be the "rip off lick guy" – learn to kick the most ass you can with your own personality!

In the next chapter you're going to take the number system to the next level and there will be plenty of cool licks to learn too.

Chapter 2 – The I Chord (G Major)

Next level Roman history

As we've seen, the harmonised major scale and the Roman numeral chord system helps us to understand how chords are formed, and how progressions are constructed. In Chapter 1 we discussed how to target specific chord tones to create lines that strongly outline the changes. Roman numeral chord numbers can also be used to help find specific scale, pentatonic or arpeggio choices that ultimately give each chord number its own "tailored" sound. Over the next few chapters we'll discuss what soloing options are available for each chord in the harmonised major scale.

All the examples are in the key of G Major. This is the parent scale from which all other scale choices are derived. Here are the diatonic chords in the key of G Major with their respective chord numbers.

Chord	G Major	A Minor	B Minor	C Major	D Major	E Minor	F#mb5
Roman Numeral	I	ii	Iii	IV	V	vi	vii

We're going to work through each chord in turn using the same process. You'll learn:

- The scale across all six strings in both three-note-per string and CAGED patterns

- The pentatonic scale relating to each chord

- The chord's triad arranged in three positions across all six strings

- The chord's seventh arpeggio (e.g. Gmaj7, Am7 etc) in three positions across all six strings

- A tasty lick for each of the above to show how you can use them in a musical context

I chord: G Major

To begin mastering the I chord, play through Example 2a. This is a G Major scale (also known as the G Ionian mode) spanning all six strings. Bar 1 is a useful three-note-per-string pattern. Bar 2 is a CAGED system scale shape.

Important disclaimer! *There is much debate about whether it's better to use three-note-per-string or CAGED shapes. It doesn't matter. Get used to both and use what works for you when improvising. Steer clear of internet arguments pertaining to this subject. It could be time better spent watching old seasons of Gilmore Girls. #teamlogan*

Example 2a:

Example 2b uses the three-note-per-string pattern but includes expressive techniques and varying subdivisions to create an interesting and musical lick.

Example 2b:

Next, I use the G Major CAGED shape, but vary the timing.

Example 2c:

The G Major Pentatonic scale is made up from five sweet G Major scale notes: G, A, B, D and E (intervals 1, 2, 3, 5 and 6). Play through the G Major Pentatonic scale in the box and horizontal shapes.

Example 2d:

The lick in Example 2e is created from the major pentatonic box shape. You'll notice at the end of the lick there's a double stop. Don't be afraid to experiment with these mini chords in your solos!

Example 2e:

Example 2f comes from the crawling pentatonic shape, played using predominantly 1/8 triplet notes.

Example 2f:

The 1, 3 and 5 intervals of the G Major scale (G, B and D) create a G Major triad. Example 2g shows how to play the triad in six- and five-string variations.

Example 2g:

Here's a lick based on the six-string triad shape. I've used multiple varying triplet subdivisions and a few diatonic notes to stop this arpeggio lick from sounding too bland.

Example 2h:

Now play through Example 2i, a lick based around the second G major triad arpeggio.

Example 2i:

Now, here's a lick that uses the third triad shape. The lick resolves to an E minor pentatonic shape reminiscent of Marty Friedman and The Scorpions.

Example 2j:

We can turn simple triads into extended arpeggios by adding the 7th interval, immediately making them more sophisticated. The G Major triad becomes a Gmaj7 arpeggio (G, B, D and F#). First play through the three maj7th arpeggios shown below.

Example 2k:

Here is a lick based on the first Gmaj7 arpeggio shape above, which also include notes from G Major Pentatonic.

Example 2l:

The second Gmaj7 lick uses 1/8 note triplets and dotted 1/8 note double-stops.

Example 2m:

Finally, here's a lick that uses varying subdivisions and a quick position shift to keep things interesting.

Example 2n:

Chapter 3 – The ii chord (A minor)

To solo over chord ii in the harmonised major scale (A minor), we play a G Major scale that begins and ends on the note A. It has all the notes of G Major, but now our focus has shifted to A minor (AKA the A Dorian mode). Example 3a shows the G Major scale starting from an A note, spanning all six strings in three-note-per-string and CAGED patterns.

Example 3a:

Example 3b shows how the three-note-per string shape translates into a lick with added legato and a final bend.

Example 3b:

In the next example, the A Dorian CAGED shape switches between 1/8 and 1/16 notes to keep timing of the lick varied and less predictable.

Example 3c:

Next, play through the box and horizontal versions of the G Major Pentatonic scale beginning from an A note to target the ii chord.

Example 3d:

Here's a lick I've created using the box shape, with varied timing and hammer-ons.

Example 3e:

Here's an example using the crawling scale shape, played with predominantly 1/8 triplet notes and resolving on a bend.

Example 3f:

The A minor chord triad consists of the notes A, C and E. Here are the six- and five-string triad patterns.

Example 3g:

Example 3h, based on the six-string shape, features a few moments of legato to add smoothness and speed.

Example 3h:

In Example 3i, legato technique is used again and is great for adding a surprise burst of speed.

Example 3i:

Here's an idea using the third triad shape played almost exclusively in 1/8 note triplets.

Example 3j:

Now we'll extend our triad to include the 7th interval to spell an Am7 arpeggio (A, C, E and G). First play through all three arpeggio shapes below.

Example 3k:

Here is a melodic line based on the first Am7 arpeggio shape.

Example 3l:

Example 3m uses the second arpeggio shape and combines 1/8 note triplets with moments of legato.

Example 3m:

Here's an idea that uses string skips to create interesting intervals and legato to create bursts of speed.

Example 3n:

Chapter 4 – The iii chord (B minor)

To solo over chord iii in the harmonised major scale (B minor), we play a G Major scale that begins and ends on the note B. It has all the notes of G Major, but now our focus has shifted to B minor (AKA the B Phrygian mode). Example 4a shows the G Major scale starting from B, spanning all six strings in three-note-per-string and CAGED patterns.

Example 4a:

The first example is based on the three-note-per-string pattern and ends with a full tone bend.

Example 4b:

This lick uses the CAGED shape, varying the timing to give the line more expression.

Example 4c:

Now we move on to the box and horizontal versions of the G Major Pentatonic scale, leading from a B note to target the iii chord (B minor).

Example 4d:

The use of 4th intervals and 1/8 note triplets help make this lick more interesting.

Example 4e:

Example 4f employs the crawling pentatonic shape with a combination of 1/16 notes and 1/4 note triplets. It concludes with a brief B minor triad arpeggio.

Example 4f:

The B minor chord triad is constructed from the notes B, D and F#. Play through the six- and five-string variations of this arpeggio.

Example 4g:

Example 4h begins with a slower 1/8 note descending arpeggio and resolves with some faster ascending 1/16 notes to add some speed and excitement.

Example 4h:

This lick based around the second B minor triad shape uses a simple descending idea with even 1/8 note timing.

Example 4i:

The lick uses varying subdivisions, slides and legato to keep things interesting.

Example 4j:

Now we extend our triad to become a 7th arpeggio (B, D, F# and A). Play through the three Bm7 arpeggios shown below.

Example 4k:

The first idea here uses repetitive building 1/16 notes to ramp up the tension ready for the release in bar two.

Example 4l:

This lick features plenty of bends to achieve its distinctive rocky edge.

Example 4m:

The final lick, based on the third Bm7 arpeggio shape, ascends using 1/8 note triplets and some quick legato.

Example 4n:

Chapter 5 – IV chord (C Major)

To solo over chord IV in the harmonised major scale (C Major), we play a G Major scale that begins and ends on the note C. It has all the notes of G Major, but now our focus has shifted to C Major (AKA the C Lydian mode). Example 5a shows the G Major scale starting from C, spanning all six strings in three-note-per-string and CAGED patterns.

Example 5a:

Example 5b features a 1/16 note line with an interesting pattern to turn an otherwise linear scale shape into something more exciting.

Example 5b:

When faced with a potentially dull scale, you can also create an interesting combination of rhythms to keep things fresh. This idea has a combination of 1/8 notes, 1/8 note triplets and 1/16th notes.

Example 5c:

Curve ball alert! For the pentatonic scale choice over the IV chord, I'm going to deviate from the pattern I've followed thus far and make an outlandish suggestion! The E Hirajoshi scale is a great pentatonic scale choice here. The notes of this Japanese pentatonic scale are E, F#, G, B and C, but when they're rearranged to start from a C note, the scale has an oriental, perhaps galactic, Lydian sound that targets the root, 3rd, #4, 5th and 7th of the IV chord.

Example 5d:

Side note: If you want to learn more about Hirajoshi and Lydian scales, you may wish to check out my second book *Rock Guitar Mode Mastery*.

Example 5e:

The C Major chord triad is constructed from the notes C, E and G. Play through the six- and five-string variations in Example 5f.

Example 5f:

In Example 5g I have juxtaposed 1/4 notes with 1/16 notes add a big variance in speed.

Example 5g:

The next example includes a brief motif from E minor Pentatonic box shape one.

Example 5h:

The lick is played using one bar of 1/4 note triplets, then a bar of 1/8 triplets, which gives the lick a progression in speed.

Example 5i:

Now we'll turn our attention to the IV chord's 7th arpeggio. Cmaj7 is constructed from the notes C, E, G and B. Play through the three major 7th arpeggios shown here.

Example 5j:

Based on the six-string arpeggio shape, this lick has several changes of direction, keeping the listener guessing about whether it's ascending or descending.

Example 5k:

This line has descending 1/16 note triplets and some slow sexy slides, with massive intervals.

Example 5l:

Finally, I use string skips in Example 5m to produce some surprising intervals, and vary between 1/16 and 1/8 note triplets to create a gradual decline in speed as the lick progresses.

Example 5m:

Chapter 6 – The V chord (D Major)

Chord V in the harmonised major scale is D Major. To improvise over it we can play a G Major scale that begins and end on the note D. It's still a G Major scale, but our focus has shifted to D Major (AKA the D Mixolydian mode). Example 6a shows the G Major scale starting from D, spanning all six strings in three-note-per-string and CAGED patterns.

Example 6a:

In Example 6b I use the three-note-per-string shape above, but include a few expressive techniques, with varying subdivisions to create an interesting and musical lick.

Example 6b:

In the next example, using the CAGED shape, the use of 1/16 notes adds an element of speed and the bend at the end of lick gives it a sense of resolution.

Example 6c:

Now play through the box and horizontal versions of the G Major Pentatonic scale, leading from the D note to targets the root of the V chord.

Example 6d:

This lick resolves on some repeating 1/8 note triplets. It's a quick reminder that you're allowed to play the same note, two or more times in a row in your solos! (Check out the solo in Motley Crue's song *Dr Feelgood*, to hear this concept executed perfectly.

Example 6e:

Example 6f uses the G major crawling pentatonic shape and a brief 1/4 note triplet D major arpeggio.

Example 6f:

For the pentatonic element in this chapter, I'm going to focus exclusively on the D Mixolydian Pentatonic scale. It has a scale formula of 1, 3, 4, 5 and b7 (D, F#, G, A and C). This scale highlights all the crucial aspects of the V chord.

Example 6g:

To demonstrate this scale, I'm playing a fast descending lick using legato and slides.

Example 6h:

The V chord (D Major) is built from the notes D, F# and A to form a D Major triad. Play through the six- and five-string variations of this arpeggio.

Example 6i:

Example 6j is a lick built from the first triad shape. It uses varying triplet subdivisions and a few diatonic notes to keep the lick fresh and sassy.

Example 6j:

The next example includes a few notes from G Major Pentatonic to resolve the lick.

Example 6k:

Here is a similar approach, borrowing a few notes from G Major Pentatonic.

Example 6l:

As before, we'll turn our triad into a 7th arpeggio to make the V chord a D7 (D, F#, A and C). Play through the three dominant 7th arpeggios shown below.

Example 6m:

Example 6n is based predominantly on 1/8 note triplets and includes some cool bends.

Example 6n:

Example 6o features a line based on the second D dominant 7th arpeggio shape and drifts between ascending and descending notes.

Example 6o:

The final example uses legato and 1/16 notes to deliver a fast 'n' fresh lick.

Example 6p:

Chapter 7 – The vi chord (E minor)

Chord vi in the harmonised major scale is E minor. To improvise over it we can play a G Major scale that begins and end on the note E. It's still a G Major scale, but our focus has shifted to E major (AKA the E Aeolian mode or E Natural minor scale). Example 7a shows the G Major scale starting from E, spanning all six strings in three-note-per-string and CAGED patterns.

Example 7a:

The first example has string skips and slow moving 1/4 note triplets to make the intervals sound less predictable.

Example 7b:

You can always use a combination of expressive techniques and varied timing to create a musical sounding lick from a simple scale.

Example 7c:

Here are the box and horizontal versions of the E Minor Pentatonic scale. It targets the root, b3rd, 5th and b7 of the E minor chord.

Example 7d:

Here's a lick using the box shape. When writing this lick I had in mind Angus Young's speed and sometimes chaotic playing style and Marty Friedman's use of tense sounding outside note. Who doesn't love an outside to inside note bend?!

Example 7e:

This example uses the crawling pentatonic shape. Be wary of the tricky hammer-ons and slides in the second bar.

Example 7f:

Let's return briefly to the Hirajoshi pentatonic scale! Here the scale formula for E Hirajoshi is 1, 2, b3, 5 and b6 (E, F#, G, B and C). This scale sounds great over a vi chord if you want to add some oriental spice to your soloing ... and who doesn't? Example 7g illustrates box and horizontal versions of this scale.

Example 7g:

Here's a medium paced lick using 1/8 and 1/8 note triplets, with a few expressive techniques to add some musicality.

Example 7h:

This next idea is played almost entirely in 1/8 note triplets and combines legato and slides to add a sexy-smoothness to its delivery.

Example 7i:

Chord vi is built from the notes E, G and B, forming an E minor triad. Play through the six- and five-string variations of this arpeggio.

Example 7j:

For the first triad example lick, I decided to use dotted 1/4 notes and a 1/2 note to make this lick a pleasantly slow one. It's good to have a few licks up you sleeve for the "calm after the storm" moments in your improvised solos.

Example 7k:

Here, however, I play predominantly 1/16 notes, because sometimes, you just gotta play fast!

Example 7l:

Example 7m mixes things up speed-wise.

Example 7m:

Now we'll turn our E minor chord into Em7 (E, G, B and D). Play through the three minor 7th arpeggios below.

Example 7n:

I've used legato here to add smoothness, as well as an inside to outside bend to give the lick a funky resolution.

Example 7o:

This next idea is relatively simple, drifting between 1/8 and 1/8 note triplets, with a few moments of cheeky legato.

Example 7p:

Lastly, a combination of 1/16 notes, legato and slides to give this lick speed and aggression.

Example 7q:

Chapter 8 – The vii chord (F#m7b5)

Chord vii in the harmonised major scale is F#m7b5. To improvise over it we can play a G Major scale that begins and end on the note F#. It's still a G Major scale, but our focus has shifted to F# minor (AKA the F# Locrian mode). Example 8a shows the G Major scale starting from F#, spanning all six strings in three-note-per-string and CAGED patterns.

Example 8a:

Our first example uses the three-note-per-string F# Locrian pattern and ends with a cheeky unison bend.

Example 8b:

As seen in previous examples, here I vary the timing and expression to create an interesting musical lick.

Example 8c:

Now we'll use the F# Locrian Pentatonic scale as our main weapon of choice. The scale formula is 1 b3 4 b5 b7 (F#, A, B, C and E). It could also be described as the F# Minor Pentatonic scale with a flattened 5th, and it works perfectly over a vii chord.

Example 8d:

This crazy lick combines legato and 1/16th notes to keep it fast and exciting.

Example 8e:

Side Note! If you want to learn more about the Locrian Pentatonic in multiple position, get hold of my book *Rock Guitar Mode Mastery*.

The vii chord triad is built from the notes F#, A and C (intervals 1, 3 and b5). Play through the six- and five-string variations of this arpeggio.

Example 8f:

The first triad lick is played in a descending manner with a cheeky outside bend.

Example 8g:

Example 8h uses 1/16th notes with an emphasis on groups of three.

Example 8h:

Here's a relatively slow lick, delivered in 1/4 note triplets for a slow, staggered effect.

Example 8i:

Our vii arpeggio is built from the notes F#, A, C and E to form an F#m7b5. Play through the three m7b5 arpeggios shown below.

48

Example 8j:

Example 8k begins with straight 1/16 notes, but uses many varying subdivisions in the second bar to throw the listener.

Example 8k:

This lick uses a lot of 1/8 notes to keep the speed manageable, and throws in a few legato notes for smoothness and speed.

Example 8l:

Lastly, here is a slow-moving 1/4 note triplet lick.

Example 8m:

Keep in mind that all of these targeted chord options are easy to modulate. They can all be moved around from key to key and are also relative in modal chord progressions too. For example. if an A Mixolydian chord progression has the chords I, bVII, IV and I those chords will be A, G, D and A, but that will also work in a theoretical sense with V, IV, I and V chord from D major as both share the same notes and chords. This means all your target chord number options will be the same, after you have done the math!

Using chord numbers together in a progression

We've worked through every chord in the harmonised major scale and learnt tons of licks, to close out this chapter I've included a couple examples of how you can apply these ideas over popular chord progressions. This is just a small taste of what is possible and you should go and practise all the ideas covered so far over some jam tracks.

First, let's look at a I V vi IV progression in G Major (G Major – D Major – E minor – C Major)

Below is a mini-solo over this progression. Here's a breakdown of melodic ideas I chose to use for each chord:

Gmaj (I): G Major triad five-string arpeggio

Dmaj (V): G Major Pentatonic scale from D (D, E, G, A and B)

Em (vi): E Acolian mode

Cmaj (IV): Cmaj7 six-string arpeggio

Example 8n:

The next example progression is a I vii ii IV progression in G Major (G Major – F#m7b5 – Am – C Major). Here's the breakdown of my melodic choices:

Gmaj (I): G Major diatonic CAGED shape

F#m7b5 (vii): F#m7b5 arpeggio, two octaves, leading from F#

Am (ii): G Major Pentatonic scale from A (A, B, D, E and G)

Cmaj (IV): C Lydian/E Hirajoshi pentatonic box

Example 80:

One final example: a vi iii IV V progression in G Major. The result of not including a G Major chord here will give the progression more of an E minor sound. Play through the example and listen to the interplay between the chords and the lead lines. Here's a breakdown of my scale choices:

Em (vi): Em7 five-string arpeggio shape

Bm (iii): B Phrygian CAGED shape

Cmaj (IV): C Major six-string triad arpeggio

Dmaj (V): D Mixolydian three-note-per-string scale shape

Example 8p:

Now that you've seen how these concepts can be applied to three common chord sequences, it's time to write some progressions of your own and to practise soloing over them. I suggest you start in the key of G Major and use your favourite licks so far. When you start to feel comfortable applying these ideas in G Major, transpose your progressions/licks to other keys.

Chapter 9 – Handling Non-Diatonic Chords

In the previous chapters we worked systematically through the diatonic chords in the harmonised G Major scale and learnt how to solo over each. Hopefully, everything made sense to you and felt "Hunky Dory" (which in Latin, I believe, means *hunky dory*).

However, many chord progressions don't contain solely diatonic chords. Chords outside of the diatonic harmony will come to visit and we'll need to adjust the way we solo over them accordingly. It's important we make these "visiting" chords welcome and ourselves sound awesome.

Non-diatonic chords can create all sorts of problems when it comes to improvisation. The sudden curveball chord can leave players puzzled and flustered. Fear not though, by the end of this chapter you'll be able to tackle them confidently.

Now, I know what you're thinking…

"This sounds like silly bogus jazz business, Christopher. I like Blues, Rock and Metal! I don't even listen to music with OUTSIDE or VISITING chords!"

I assure you that lots of the music you listen to features non-diatonic chords. They're often used to create an element of surprise to grab the listener's attention. Since the Beatles rise to fame, non-diatonic chords have been widely accepted in contemporary pop music. Let's look at an example.

The progression is Example 9a is the same as the first four bars of *Creep* by Radiohead. The chords are G Major, B Major, C Major and C minor. The G Major and C Major chords are diatonic to G Major; the B Major and C minor chords are non-diatonic. In Roman numerals we'd write the progression like this: I III IV ivm.

In G Major, the iii chord is B minor. Here it has been changed to B Major, so is designated III rather than iii in numerals to indicate it's a major chord type. B Major has a D# note in it, which is non-diatonic to the key of G major.

The IV chord in G Major is C Major, but in the last bar has been changed to C minor, so is designated iv (sometimes written ivm) rather than IV to indicate it's a minor chord type. C minor has a D#/Eb note in it, which is non-diatonic to the key of G Major.

Example 9a:

"Well, what do we do now, Christopher?" I hear you ask. We ADAPT! For the rest of this chapter we're going to look at common non-diatonic chords that frequently pop up in the key of G Major (including the two pesky examples we've just discussed) and discover what we can play over them.

III/III7 chord: B major/B7

In the key of G Major, the non-diatonic III chord is a major chord (B Major) but is also frequently played as a dominant chord (B7).

B Major has just one note different to B minor. This is useful to know because we want to focus on any notes that fall outside our original key signature.

B minor (iii chord) = B D F#

B Major (III chord) = B D# F#

The key of G Major has only one sharp (F#), so it's the D# note that will cause us grief if we're not prepared. What scale can we play to take account of this non-diatonic note? The B Phrygian Dominant and B Mixolydian Pentatonic scales are both great choices.

B Phrygian Dominant = B C D# E F# G A

B Mixolydian Pentatonic = B D# E F# A

Play a B Major or B7 chord, then play through the B Phrygian Dominant scale below. I've arranged it across all six strings in a three-note-per-string shape.

Example 9b:

Let's hear how we can use this in a creative lick:

Example 9c:

Play a B Major or B7 chord again, then play through the B Mixolydian Pentatonic scale below.

Example 9d:

Here's a lick using this idea which includes an expressive bend.

Example 9e:

B Phrygian Dominant is the fifth mode of E Harmonic minor (i.e. if you take the E Harmonic minor scale and harmonise it like we did the major scale, the scale built from the *fifth* degree is B Phrygian Dominant. It's just like playing an E Harmonic minor scale beginning and ending on the note B).

It's a common technique to superimpose different scales over a chord to achieve a specific effect. Because of the B Major chord's relationship to E Harmonic minor, we can play a custom Harmonic minor pentatonic scale over it as illustrated in Example 9d. I like to call it a Pentamonic!

The scale formula is 1 b3 4 5 7 (E, G, A, B and D#).

If we play these notes beginning and ending on B, we get the pentatonic shape below, which works perfectly over the III chord.

Example 9f:

Here's a lick that uses the scale to double back on itself as it crosses the fretboard.

Example 9g:

The next most obvious way to deal with the major III chord is to use dominant arpeggios. Played over a regular V chord, dominant arpeggios will sound very safe. Played over the major III chord, however, they suddenly take on an exotic, almost Flamenco/Egyptian-like sound (apologies for mashing together two distinct cultures there without so much as a by your leave!)

Play through the three B7 arpeggios shapes shown below. Each will work well over the III chord.

Example 9h:

Here's a lick that illustrates a cool arpeggio-based line. Work through each of these three shapes and invent your own.

Example 9i:

The B Augmented arpeggio is also a good choice because it contains the notes B, D# and G. These notes correspond with the 1st, 3rd and 6th notes of the B Phrygian Dominant scale. Augmented arpeggios are moveable shapes, so you can in fact play a B Augmented, D# Augmented or G Augmented arpeggio and they'll all achieve the same effect – they all contain the same three notes, and they all sound great over a B7 chord.

Example 9j:

The augmented arpeggio is ideal for creating angular-sounding ideas like this one.

Example 9k:

Side Note: Give some time to experimenting with augmented arpeggios – they are dreadfully underrated compared to diminished arpeggios (which are used frequently in metal – core, tech, death, thrash, power etc) – neo-classical shred and flamenco). The great thing about augmented arpeggios is that they create an element of surprise to the listener – a bit of Gypsy Jazz flavour for your rock/metal playing!

Below is a mini-solo that shows how you can handle the III chord in musical context. Example 9l is a vi V IV III progression in the key of G Major/E minor. Pay close attention to the III chord. Here's a summary of what I decided to play over each chord:

Em (vi): E minor triad arpeggio

D (V): D7 arpeggio paired with a tiny section of the G Major three-note-per-string scale shape

C (IV): C Lydian three-note-per-string scale shape

B7 (III): B Phrygian Dominant three-note-per-string shape

Example 91:

iv chord: C minor

In the key of G Major, the iv chord is usually C Major. The common non-diatonic alternative is to change this to a C minor. The iv minor chord appears in many popular songs (that usually play the C Major first, then change it to a C minor), such as *When September Ends* by Green Day and *In My Life* by The Beatles.

Let's compare the iv minor to the standard IV chord:

C Major (IV) = C E G

C minor (iv) = C Eb G

The Eb (or D#) in the C minor chord is the note to look out for.

The perfect scale to accommodate this chord is C Dorian.

C Dorian = C D Eb F G A Bb

The scale has three notes that don't appear in the key of G Major (so don't go playing it over a G chord!). However, over C minor it sounds great.

Here's C Dorian arranged in as a three-note-per-string scale.

Example 9m:

Now here is how you can apply this scale in a lick over C minor.

Example 9n:

Example 9o shows the box and vertical shapes of the C minor Pentatonic scale, which of course will work swimmingly over our C minor chord. Remember you can use any of the five minor pentatonic shapes, so go and experiment.

Example 9o:

Here's an idea that makes great use of hammer-ons / pull-offs.

Example 9p:

As we've done with every other chord so far, we can attack the iv minor chord with straight-up minor triad arpeggios. Play through the three shapes below.

Example 9q:

Now here's a lick that puts these ideas to work.

Example 9r:

Let's add the 7th interval to turn the triads into minor 7th arpeggios.

Example 9s:

Example 9t uses the third arpeggio shape.

Example 9t:

Now let's see how these ideas work in a mini-solo over a I iii IV iv progression in the key of G Major. Pay close attention to the iv chord. Here's breakdown of the ideas I used:

G (I): G Major Pentatonic scale (high octave)

Bm (iii): B minor five-string arpeggio shape

C (IV): C Lydian three-note-per-string scale shape

Cm (iv): C minor descending six-string arpeggio

Example 9u:

VI/VI7 chord: E Major/E7

There are two more non-diatonic chords that crop up in the key of G Major. Here's the first! We would expect the vi chord in G Major to be an E minor. This frequently gets turned into an E Major or E7 chord. The VI7 chord is commonly found in jazz, but can work in any genre. Here's how the diatonic/non-diatonic chords compare:

E minor (vi): E G B

E Major (VI): E G# B

This time we've got a G# note to contend with, so our licks will sound particularly heinous if we take this next idea anywhere near a G Major chord. You have been warned!

Brace yourself. A great scale choice to play over the VI/VI7 chord is the E Hindu Mixolydian scale. "What the crap is that, Chris?!" I hear you cry. Trust me, you'll love it. What has been coined the "Hindu Mixolydian" is the fifth mode of the Melodic Minor scale. Its scale formula is 1 2 3 4 5 b6 b7. It is also sometimes known as the Mixolydian b6 scale and sounds excellent over the non-diatonic VI chord.

Example 9v:

How might this exotic scale sound in lick form? Here's an example.

Example 9w:

"How come this works, Chris?" I hear you ask. E Major/E7 is the V chord in the key of A Major. Viewing the VI7 chord as the V chord from A Major means we can play the mode associated with it – E Mixolydian. Here's a useful shape that maps out an E Mixolydian Pentatonic scale.

Example 9x:

65

And here's a lick that puts it to work over the E Major/E7 chord.

Example 9y:

Now let's approach the VI7 chord with E7 arpeggios as shown in Example 9z.

Example 9z:

Here's a lick that uses these arpeggios over an E7 chord.

Example 9z1:

What other scale choices might sound cool over this chord? In Example 9z2 I use the whole tone scale (which contains the notes E, F#, G#, A#, C and D). It's got the all-important G# note we need to accommodate, but the other intervals help produce a cartoon-like effect – that thing they do in movies where someone is being hypnotised, falling asleep or entering a dream sequence. It's the fact that all the notes are a tone apart that give it its spacey effect.

The whole tone scale can create outside quirkiness on any dominant 7th chord, but I think it sounds particularly cool on VI7 chords. Check out the solo in the song *Silent Wars* by Arch Enemy. There's a whole tone run of death at 2:50. Enjoy!

Example 9z2:

Here's just one example of how you might use the scale in a real-life situation.

Example 9z3:

Now let's put some of these ideas into a mini-solo. Example 9z4 is a ii V I VI7 progression in the key of G Major. Here's a summary of what I played over it.

Am (ii): G Major Pentatonic scale shape two

D (V): D7 arpeggio

G (I): G Major three-note-per-string scale shape

E7 (VI7): Descending E Augmented arpeggio

Example 9z4:

vii Diminished 7 chord: F#dim7

Lastly, the non-diatonic viidim7 chord can easily be mistaken for the diatonic vii chord – but the non-diatonic chord is diminished, whereas the diatonic chord is a m7b5.

In other words, in the context of the key of G Major, the non-diatonic viidim7 chord is F#dim7 and not the expected F#m7b5. The F#dim7 chord contains one outside note. Let's compare the two:

F#m7b5 (vii): F# A C E

F#dim7 (viidim7): F# A C D#

F#dim7 contains a D# note which is not in the key of G Major. The quickest way to deal with this chord is simply by playing an F#dim7 arpeggio. Here are two useful shapes for this in five- and six-string patterns.

Example 9z5:

Here's an idea based on these shapes.

Example 9z6:

What makes diminished 7th chords special is that the notes they contain are all spaced a minor third apart. This means that can easily be inverted and moved around. All the notes are the same, just in a different order. All the arpeggios below will therefore work over the viidim7 chord. (D#dim7, F#dim7, Adim7 and Cdim7).

In Example 9z7 the same five-string arpeggio shape is played in four different positions to achieve this effect.

Example 9z7:

Here's a lick that combines some of these shapes.

Example 9z8:

Alternatively, we can use the Diminished Scale over the viidim7 chord. This is sometimes called the half-whole or whole-half scale. The intervals are played as a whole step followed by a half step in a repeating pattern or vice versa. Play through both variations of the F# Diminished Scale below as a three-note-per-string pattern, spanning five strings.

Example 9z9:

Here's a creative lick that moves freely through the two patterns.

Example 9z10:

A final scale choice is the F# Locrian Natural 6th Scale. OK, that's a lot of information right there. The Locrian mode is the seventh mode of the major scale and designed to fit over m7b5 chords. Since our viidim7 chord has one note different to the m7b5 chord, we're adjusting one note. It's a Locrian scale with a natural 6th instead of a b6.

Example 9z11:

Here's a cool, angular-sounding lick using the scale.

Example 9z12:

Here's a I IV vi viidim7 progression in the key of G Major and an accompanying mini-solo. Here's the usual breakdown of what I decided to play:

G (I): G Major Pentatonic scale in a horizontal crawling shape

C (IV): Cmaj7 arpeggio plus E Hirajoshi scale fragment

Em (vi): E Minor Pentatonic

F#dim7 (viidim7): F#dim7 arpeggio and a descending diminished scale

Example 9z13:

I thought I'd end this viidim7 section in Jerry Springer style, like a *Jerry's final thoughts* reflection. Diminished chords are tricky things, but as you've seen, there are more creative ways to play over them than sweeping a diminished arpeggio. Keep things interesting with multiple approaches. Then, and only then, will you be the coolest kid in the playground… it's never too late to prove those jerks wrong!

Chapter 10 – Soloing Using Chords & Breaking Out of the Single Note Box

So far, you've encountered a huge number of licks that can be played over diatonic and non-diatonic chords. But single line solos and motifs should not be the only weapon in your melodic improvisation arsenal. "What else is there besides cool single note licks, Christopher?" I hear you ask.

That's the subject matter and rabbit hole we'll concern ourselves with next. In this chapter you'll learn how to use chordal concepts and combine them to great effect with your single line soloing. We'll cover major and minor 3rds, 4ths, 5ths, 6ths and "bleeding note" arpeggiated chords.

This chapter also heralds a change of key and all the examples will be based around the G Dorian mode.

Thirds

The G Dorian scale is built from the notes G A Bb C D E F. It is the second mode of the key of F Major (like playing an F Major scale, beginning and ending on the note G).

For starters, we're going to take the G Dorian scale (or mode if you prefer) and play through the scale using major and minor thirds. This is the simplest, most rudimentary introduction to using chords (chord fragments in this case) in your solos. But, when used tastefully, 3rd-based chords can create some cheeky motifs in your lead playing.

Play through the following example.

Example 10a:

If we were to harmonise the G Dorian scale like we did the major scale, we'd get the following chords:

Gm7 – Am7 – Bbmaj7 – C7 – Dm7 – Ebm7b5 – Fmaj7

In Example 10a, the lower pitched note is the root note of these chords. The higher pitched note is either a minor or major third, accordingly:

Root note:	G	A	Bb	C	D	E	F
3rd above:	Bb	C	D	E	F	G	A
Interval:	b3	b3	3	3	b3	b3	3

Here's how chord fragments like this can work used as part of a lick.

Example 10b:

Fourths

Compared with the mellow sounding thirds, fourths have a harder-edged, more powerful sound. Play through the G Dorian scale with these 4th interval chords.

Example 10c:

Let's look at the root note/interval relationship again:

Root note:	F	G	A	Bb	C	D	E
4th above:	Bb	C	D	E	F	G	A
Interval:	4	4	4	#4	4	4	4

With the exception of the #4 interval between Bb and E, the rest of this diatonic chord 4th scale is in perfect 4th intervals.

The first bar of Example 10d uses 4ths in a sliding, riff-like motif, then works its way into a lick based around a Gm7add13 arpeggio.

Example 10d:

The 4th interval itself is not as emotionally driven as the major/minor 3rd sound, so you won't likely use it as a means to accentuate joy or sadness. I mostly use it as testosterone driven, Rock n' Roll garnish.

Plenty of great riffs have been written using 4ths (*Money For Nothing* by Dire Straits and *Smoke on the Water* by Deep Purple spring to mind). Their purpose is usually to establish a rockin' vibe.

The perfect 4th chord can all be used to get a Hendrixian or Steve Vai-esque sound. There's quite a number of sexy 4th chords in the emotive Steve Vai ballad, *Sisters*.

Fifths

One might wonder, "Why in the name of the Holy Honey Badger would I play power chords in my solo?". And in most instances, you'd have received a round of applause and a signed glossy of Argentinian-born, NBA superstar Manu Ginobli. However, today we're going to explore the 5th interval (AKA power chord) as a tool for lead guitar playing.

Here's the G Dorian scale played with 5th interval chords.

Example 10e:

Root note:	G	A	Bb	C	D	E	F
5th above:	D	E	F	G	A	Bb	C
Interval:	5	5	5	5	5	b5	5

As an ascending scale, 5ths leave little to the imagination. It reminds me of one of my least favourite INXS songs, *Don't Change*. But we're going to use it in more of a soloing manner. In the first bar of the example lick below, I use building 5th interval chords to transition into an Em7b5 arpeggio. The coarse and unmelodic nature of the 5ths is immediately juxtaposed by the melodic and jazzy arpeggio.

Example 10f:

Like 4ths, 5th chords do not yield instantaneous emotion. Quite the opposite. They can sound robotic unless used in the right place – the right place being the introduction to Jimi Hendrix's *Castles Made of Sand*, for instance, or even *CAFO* by Animals As Leaders. 5ths can add a layer mystique and awesomeness, so don't be shy. Get the 5th chord involved in your soloing but use wisely!

Sixths

Like 3rds, 6ths will be major or minor, depending on the chord. This means that we can use these chords as a means to highlight the joyous and more melancholy sounds of a chord progression.

Play though the G Dorian scale with major and minor 6ths.

Example 10g:

Root note:	G	A	Bb	C	D	E	F
6th above:	E	F	G	A	Bb	C	D
Interval:	6	b6	6	6	b6	b6	6

You can hear 6th chords like these in twelve bar blues turnarounds, as well as the delightful intro to *Wanted Dead Or Alive* by Bon Jovi.

You can hear the signature Slash 6th chords, similar to those in Example 10h, in songs like *Night Train* and *Welcome To The Jungle*.

Example 10h:

Octaves

If you ever watch me improvise on any of my YouTube videos, you'll notice I use octave chords quite a lot. They sound great in a funky George Benson context, a mystical Steve Vai context, or even a fist-raising Smashing Pumpkins rock context. The great thing about an octave chord is that you're playing the same note twice in different registers, making any melody you're playing sound twice as significant.

Example 10i shows all the octave chords in G Dorian to one octave starting on a Bb. In the song *Killing in the Name* by Rage Against The Machine, the build-up and climax into the timeless "F*** you, I won't do what you tell me!" section is created by ascending octave chords. You can also hear the building octave, climax effect in the Foo Fighters songs *Best of You*, *My Hero*, *Everlong* and *The Pretender*.

Example 10i:

In Example 10j, I play octave chords from the 1st string to the 5th and blend it with a fragment of a Gm7add13 arpeggio.

Example 10j:

Unison bends

Connected to this idea of doubling up notes, unison bends can really cement a melodic idea. A unison bend begins with two notes a tone apart played simultaneously. The lower of the two is then bent until both notes are the same.

In Example 10k I begin with E and D notes. The D is bent a full tone and we end up with two E notes in the same register, creating a slightly wobbly chorus effect.

Play through this G Dorian scale to one octave, using unison bends, starting and ending on an E note.

Example 10k:

In Example 10l, I've used unison bends to highlight D, F and E (the 5th, minor 7th and major 6th of the G Dorian scale). The line resolves on a triplet run using the 1st and 2nd strings from the G Dorian three-note-per-string shape.

Example 10l:

You can hear the excellent use of unison bends by Jimmy Page in the outro to *Stairway To Heaven* by Led Zeppelin. The slow ascending bends create a brooding tension and build up to the song's final climax.

Josh Homme from Queens of The Stone Age and Kyuss has been using unison bends his whole career, as a staple of his lead guitar approach. He often uses them in a fast, abrasive, staccato manner in order to somewhat attack the listener.

I've always loved how much impact a unison bend can have when played slowly. It can sound abrasive and huge! They will also encourage you, the player, to slow down and not constantly fill your phrases with a bajillion notes.

Sustained (or bleeding) arpeggiated chords

Another great chordal technique can be achieved through the use of arpeggios. Rather than play a "clean" arpeggio, we can hold the notes and allow them to "bleed" into each other. Jerry Cantrell uses this concept in several Alice in Chains solos and some of his solo projects. The solo in *Anger Rising* has some great sustained chord arpeggiations.

Josh Middleton from Sylosis uses this concept in countless solos. There's a few beautiful examples of sustained chord arpeggiations at the beginning of the solo in *Eclipsed*.

Example 10m has a chord progression of Gm, F and C. Here I play sustained arpeggio triads over each chord change.

Example 10m:

We can take this idea further by using slightly more complex arpeggiated chord voicings. In Example 10n, instead of basic triads, I play a Gm7, Fmaj9 and C7.

Example 10n:

One of the coolest things about playing lead guitar with chords and arpeggiations is that it prevents us from stuffing our solos with wild shredding, sweeping and crazy legato… well, most of the time. Holding rigid chord shapes to play arpeggiated ideas slows us down and forces us to be more measured. This is effective when juxtaposed against a climatic 1/16th triplet shred-passage-of-destiny. Played one after the other you get the excitement of chaos followed by the calm after the storm.

There are so many places where you can use chords in your soloing. The key is experimentation. Work on adding more dynamics into your solos and figuring out ways to make chordal concepts part of your lead guitar tool kit.

Chapter 11 – Varying Scales & Shred Sequences

So far, we have covered a lot of sonic territory together. You've learnt how to analyse and play over the common diatonic chords that will frequently occur in songs, plus how to tackle the non-diatonic ones. You've also learnt how to mix things up with chordal ideas. Of course, you've learnt lots of cool lick ideas along the way, but all that groundwork has been *preparation for improvisation.*

Sometimes players think that to improvise means that ideas will suddenly appears from nowhere, falling out of the sky. The truth is, all the hard work that goes into preparation is what gives you the ability to be spontaneous.

But still, the threat remains, with the scale and arpeggio knowledge you've gained, that your melodic ideas can sound clichéd. When I first plunged into the world of improvisation, I found myself constantly falling into the robotic delivery of scales, arpeggios and shred sequences. Everything I played sounded "up and down". It was hardly memorable. My improvisation lacked *pizazz.*

From one gangsta to another, there's nothing more offensive than hearing a guitarist trying to find their own expressive voice, playing solos that sound like exercises straight out of a scale book.

This chapter, then, is solely devoted to teaching you different approaches to soloing with common scales, so that they sound sexy, less linear. This will lead you into a truer expression of your personality as musician.

All the examples in this chapter are demonstrated in the key of B minor. You can also jam to your heart's content over the B minor backing track included in the free download.

Pentatonic Sequences

The pentatonic scale is definitely the most popular in the world of guitar soloing. As a result, it's also the most likely to sound scale and predictable in the wrong hands. However, in the hands of a musician who has exciting tools and approaches at their disposal it can sound super interesting and sexy.

Let's begin by playing B Minor Pentatonic in its simplest ascending form.

Example 11a:

To help avoid sounding routine, we could first add some rhythm and play with a triplet pulse. You may have heard pentatonic sequences like this being played by Kirk Hammett and Ace Frehley. This is a common way to add speed and variance to the pentatonic shape.

Example 11b:

We can also use B minor Pentatonic in four-note groupings with a 1/16th note pulse. This approach is used by blues guitar greats like Eric Johnson and Joe Bonamassa.

Example 11c:

Now here's something a little different. B minor Pentatonic played in five-note groupings and with a 1/16th note pulse. When played with a backing track, you'll hear that the phrasing of the scale lands in some pretty interesting places, making it less predictable to the listener. This approach to pentatonic playing is reminiscent of virtuosic players like Guthrie Govan and Shawn Lane.

Example 11d:

The next example breaks up the pentatonic scale into jumps of predominantly 4ths, with an occasional major 3rd interval thrown in for good measure. This intervallic approach to playing the pentatonic scale creates a very different sound to the pentatonic clichés one might expect.

Example 11e:

The following pentatonic line uses predominantly 5th and some minor 6th intervals. Stacking multiple 5th intervals on top of each other can create a galactic, space adventure vibe, reminiscent of virtuoso Steve Vai. A perfect example of this is the bridge section of his song *Die to Live*.

Example 11f:

Example 11g has an ascending idea with string skips. This is a simple way to create large intervallic jumps and create an element of surprise for the listener.

Example 11g:

Here's another descending triplet pentatonic idea, but this time it includes string skips!

Example 11h:

You could use the string skip idea with *any* of the concepts we've discussed in this book, to vary how they are played and avoid sounding like you're running up and down scales.

Try each of these pentatonic ideas in all five positions of the pentatonic scale in various keys.

Diatonic Shred and Legato Sequences

Diatonic, three-note-per-string scales can sound incredibly dull and robotic if applied without creativity. This section is devoted to making these scale shapes sound interesting and less predictable. We'll use the B Aeolian (AKA B Natural Minor) scale throughout, but you should practise these ideas with different scales, shapes and keys.

Here's a three-note-per-string B Aeolian scale shape covering all six strings.

Example 11i:

An easy way to break up the linear nature of the scale is to play it in intervals. Here it is arranged with 3rd interval jumps.

Example 11j:

If you come up with a great idea, always play it ascending and descending.

Example 11k:

The next idea has the B Aeolian scale arranged in groups of four notes ascending and descending. This approach to shredding can be heard in Alex Skolnick's solo in the Testament masterpiece *Apocalyptic City.*

The descending version of this idea has more of a hair metal sound to it. Players like Satchel (Steel Panther) and CC Deville (Poison) use this pattern in countless solos.

Example 11l:

Ascending B Aeolian building 16ths

Descending B Aeolian building 16ths

Here is a B Aeolian "double triplet" shred idea. Matt Heafy and Corey Beaulieu from Trivium use this approach in the solos on *Into The Mouth Of Hell We March* and *In The Fire*.

Example 11m:

Ascending B Aeolian Speed Double Triplets

Descending B Aeolian Speed Double Triplets

Here's an interesting B Aeolian three-note-per-string shape that uses legato and a five-note pulse. Unpredictable pulses and note groupings are a great way of keeping shred and legato passages unpredictable.

Example 11n:

Here's a similar legato idea, but this time the notes are grouped in sevens. Rolling in triplets with a sevens pulse is pretty weird, so be patient if you're trying to lock in with music or a metronome.

Example 11o:

The next creative idea is a Neoclassical three-note-per-string concept that's used by players like Yngwie Malmsteen, Jason Becker and Michael Romeo. It gives these shapes a violin-esque sound, reminiscent of the playing style and compositions of Paganini and Vivaldi.

Each string has four picked notes which allows you to keep your picking consistent across all six strings. This makes the picking pattern less confusing, as string changes and 1/16th note playing on three-note-per-string patterns can be quite difficult.

Example 11p:

Ascending B Aeolian Neoclassical

Descending B Aeolian Neoclassical

The next idea is formed from a three-note triad built on each note of the scale. This means that every three notes form the triads of Bm, C#m7b5, D Major, Em, F#m, G Major and A Major in sequence. It's a powerful approach and shows that triads don't just have to be used for chord targeting.

Example 11q:

Ascending B Aeolian 3 note arpeggios

Descending B Aeolian 3 note arpeggios

Now play through this B Aeolian three-note-per-string shape with added string skips. This is not only fun to play creates some interesting intervallic jumps.

Example 11r:

In Example 11s I demonstrate a combination of the string skipped legato and the five-note-per-string rolling legato from earlier examples.

Example 11s:

Remember that everything discussed in this section can be transferred to any key, and any three-note-per-string scale. You can transfer these ideas to G Lydian, F Dorian or even an E Hungarian Minor three-note-per-string scale shape! Get creative and try them out in a few different contexts.

More Interesting Arpeggio Sequences

In the final section of this chapter, we'll look at the two most common, five-string arpeggio shapes and how to rearrange them to sound more interesting. All examples use a B minor / D Major triad pattern. First, learn then both in their simplest ascending form.

Example 11t:

In the first example, both arpeggios are made more interesting by skipping every second note to create a less linear sequential line.

Example 11u:

Now try playing the B minor and D Major arpeggio with gradually ascending 1/8th note triplets. This simple approach makes a six-note, two-octave arpeggio, that is twelve notes in length.

Example 11v:

B Minor Building Arpeggio Triplets

D Major Building Arpeggio Triplets

In this final example, each note of the arpeggio is followed by a 5th interval to create a less predictable melody with a futuristic, power chord-esque vibe.

Example 11w:

B Minor Arpeggio w/ascending 5ths

D Major Arpeggio w/ascending 5ths

Remember that any of these arpeggio concepts can be used on any triad and any major 7th, minor 7th, dominant 7th, diminished or augmented arpeggio.

This book isn't designed to be a thesaurus of arpeggio shapes, but merely to plant the seed of creative approaches you can use on any arpeggio in an improvised or written solo.

Chapter 12 – Adding Even More Flair, Sass & Pizazz

What makes Slash, Hugh Jackman and Shania Twain infinitely·cooler than all of us? Well I guess I could narrow it down to three things: *flair, sass* and *pizazz!*

I bet you're thinking, "Those are dumb buzz words, Chris! What am I going to do with that?" and you'd be right.

Let's put it a different way. How can you add cool techniques to your playing that make it more exciting? That give it a creative edge? In this chapter we'll add the icing on the cake and discuss how to achieve this by using bends, slides and legato. I'm also going to throw in some cheeky grace notes and the odd "outside" note. All of which will add up to make you stand out from the crowd as a player.

Add Flair with Bends

One of the things that really sets the guitar apart as an instrument is the ability to bend notes in order to create emotion and expression. How we bend notes and add vibrato to them is so personal that many players can immediately be identified just by playing a couple of notes. Here are a few cool bending ideas you should incorporate into your playing right away.

In Example 12a I use three bends to transition from shape three to shape one of the E Minor Pentatonic scale. This concept is not limited to pentatonic scales, of course, and can be used to shift to different positions of any scale or arpeggio.

Example 12a:

The next idea uses a five-string E minor triad arpeggio with a tense, outside bend from the b5 (Bb) to 5 (B). What's not to love about an outside-to-inside bend?

Example 12b:

Here's an E Hirajoshi lick with an outside bend from an F (b2) to F# (natural 2). The b2 has a tense Phrygian sound until it resolves into the bent natural 2nd. The release bend in the second bar helps the lick resolve in a pleasing manner.

Example 12c:

Here's an E minor Pentatonic lick using shapes one and two. It capitalises on a tense outside bend from a major 3rd to perfect 4th in two octaves. You can always milk a bend by playing it slowly!

Example 12d:

In the final example I use bends to descend the fretboard through multiple shapes of E minor Pentatonic. The large interval jumps and position shifts are not only impressive to watch, but add a bonus of 40% to your total flair score from the Norwegian judge.

Example 12e:

Add Sass with Slides

Like bends, you can also use slides as a means of creating tension. They are ideal to help you shift position and, of course, the old Zoupa favourite – to add interesting outside notes.

Here's an E minor Pentatonic idea with two slides from the b5 to perfect 5th, played on the B string.

Example 12f:

Example 12g has a two octave E minor triad arpeggio with a slide from the major 7th to root, and the b5 to perfect 5th. This approach adds tension to any arpeggio at the entry point, midway, or at the end. You should also experiment with this concept on major, augmented and diminished arpeggios.

Example 12g:

This next idea uses a six-note A Dorian shape ascending three octaves. This lick includes slides from an outside F note (b2) into an inside F# note (2). This approach works well on any six-note scale shape.

Example 12h:

The next example features a variation on a standard jazzy chromatic run, commonly referred to as "the lick". The outside slides create a tension between the b2 and the regular 2nd and also between the b5 and perfect 5th. Well placed chromaticism is a great way to add quintessentially jazzy flair to metal and rock soloing.

Example 12i:

Next is an E minor Pentatonic played across two strings with outside note slides to create multiple position shifts. The horizontal slides add visual flair, but also have a less linear melodic delivery.

Example 12j:

Cheeky Outside Legato Pizazz

A sprinkle of well-placed legato will always create tension, unexpected bursts of speed, interesting outside note usage and, most importantly, *pizazz*.

Play through this E minor Pentatonic fragment that descends through shape three. Speed is created with the placement of legato 1/16th triplets while the lick also highlights the tense, outside b5 note.

Example 12k:

Here's another take on this idea that includes the outside sounding b5.

Example 12l:

Example 12m features a G Major idea, similar to the previous example, that highlights the b5 and major 7th for another morsel of "outside note goodness".

Side Note: I just coined that term… still not sure if I'm fond of it.

Example 12m:

Next is a five-string E minor triad arpeggio with triplet 1/16ths and grace notes to create tension on the b5 and the major 7th. This approach adds an element of Gypsy Jazz to the sound of an otherwise overused, meat and veg arpeggio shape.

Example 12n:

In the next example I demonstrate a pentatonic idea that moves horizontally over three octaves. The outside legato is played as a grace note to create a burst of tension and resolve between the b5 and the perfect 5th. There's also a major 7th interval played with grace notes on the final octave (because when in Rome, right girlfriends?)

Example 12o:

Hopefully, this chapter has stimulated some creative ideas you can apply right away to the licks you know. It's amazing what mileage you can get out of a pretty standard lick by adding a healthy dose of flair, sass and pizazz.

Remember, these ideas are not key specific. Try them in other keys and intertwine the different techniques to create your own individual, unique flair, sass and pizazz to your improvisations.

Chapter 13 – Writing a Solo and Bringing it all Together

We've covered so much territory in this book that it's impossible to pack all of those ideas into ONE solo. I had to be selective – and yet, this is what I'll attempt to do now!

In order to get better at improvisation, in the beginning it's fine to have a plan – even a rough map of the territory you intend to cover. Learning how to structure and a solo with your composition head on will not only aid your song writing, but also your improvisation.

In this last chapter I'm going to give you a run down on how to structure a guitar solo help you think about how you can write your own. I'll include as many elements as possible from the previous chapters.

If you think of some of the greatest solos of all time, whether they were composed or improvised, they all have a *storytelling* element to them that makes them memorable and takes the listener on a journey. What does storytelling have to do with guitar solos? Let's take look at the tale of *Little Red Riding Hood* in the most concise manner possible. Bear with me…

Beginning: Little girl decides to venture into the woods to visit Grandma.

Middle Part 1: Girl encounters wolf; politely sidesteps being eaten and continues on her way.

Middle Part 2: Wolf goes to Grandma's house and eats her, then poorly disguises himself in her bed to ready himself for a second helping of person.

Ending: Girl finds out Granny had been eaten, yells "Wolf!" till woodsman comes and slays the wolf.

This story has a beginning, and end, and a two-part double-jeopardy middle section. This exactly how I try to write my guitar solos. An obvious beginning, an interesting dual-faceted middle and a climatic or resolved ending. With that thought process in mind, have a look at the solo I've created for you to learn.

I have used the key of F# minor as the backing to the solo.

Beginning: The First Four Bars

The beginning of a solo should set the tone for things to come without giving away too much too soon.

I use 1/4 notes and dotted 1/4 notes in the first two bars to keep the melody slow and simple as well as highlighting the chord tones of the F#m. In the third bar I use 1/4 note triplets to superimpose a Dmaj7 arpeggio over the Bm chord, then I build speed using F# minor Pentatonic shape five with 1/16th notes and hammer-ons.

Example 13a:

Middle Part 1: Bars 5-8

In this section of the solo, I want the story to progress a bit further and add some tension to keep the story exciting and the listener engaged.

Using the momentum built from bar four, I continue the F# minor Pentatonic run through bars five and six, nearly playing in strict 1/16th notes with an initial triplet and a few 1/8th notes.

In bar seven, I use an outside to inside bend to target the root note of the Bm chord. I also use some double-stop chords as a contrast to all the single note lines that have been played so far. I resolve the final bar on some slow notes from F# minor Pentatonic shape three.

Example 13b:

Middle Part 2: Bars 9-12

In the majority of my solos, this is the point at which I'll bring the most chaos and aim for a climactic peak. You'll notice that these next four bars have more notes than any of the other sections.

The ninth bar begins with a 1/16th rest, then works into a combination of an F#m7 arpeggio with a superimposed Amaj7 arpeggio. This bar is made entirely of 1/16th notes and heads towards a tapped pentatonic on bar ten. This is played with 1/16th triplets to create another shift in gear.

Example 13c:

Ending: The Last Four Bars

To end this solo, I decided to pull back from the chaos a little to give the solo dynamics and varying moments of intensity.

In the first bar, over the F#m chord, I play a simple F# minor Pentatonic lick beginning with an outside grace note. I then work into a simple octave chord melody using 1/4 note triplets to add a staggered, minimalist sound.

In bar 15, over the Bm chord, I leave ample space at the beginning of the bar, then pick up with a lick based around F# minor Pentatonic shape three.

Over the A chord in bar 16 I use the A Ionian three-note-per-string shape with a neoclassical picking pattern. I then turn the lick into a mixture of legato and shred, increasing the speed by using 1/16th and 1/32 triplets.

Example 13d:

Listen to the backing track provided and try to create your own solo. You can use my soloing guide as a structure to create your own, but experimentation is the name of the game. Break all the rules and do whatever you want to do! Try drawing at least one idea from every chapter in your solo composition!

The following pages feature the notation/TAB for the entire solo. You can listen to it on audio Example 13e included with the free download.

Full Solo

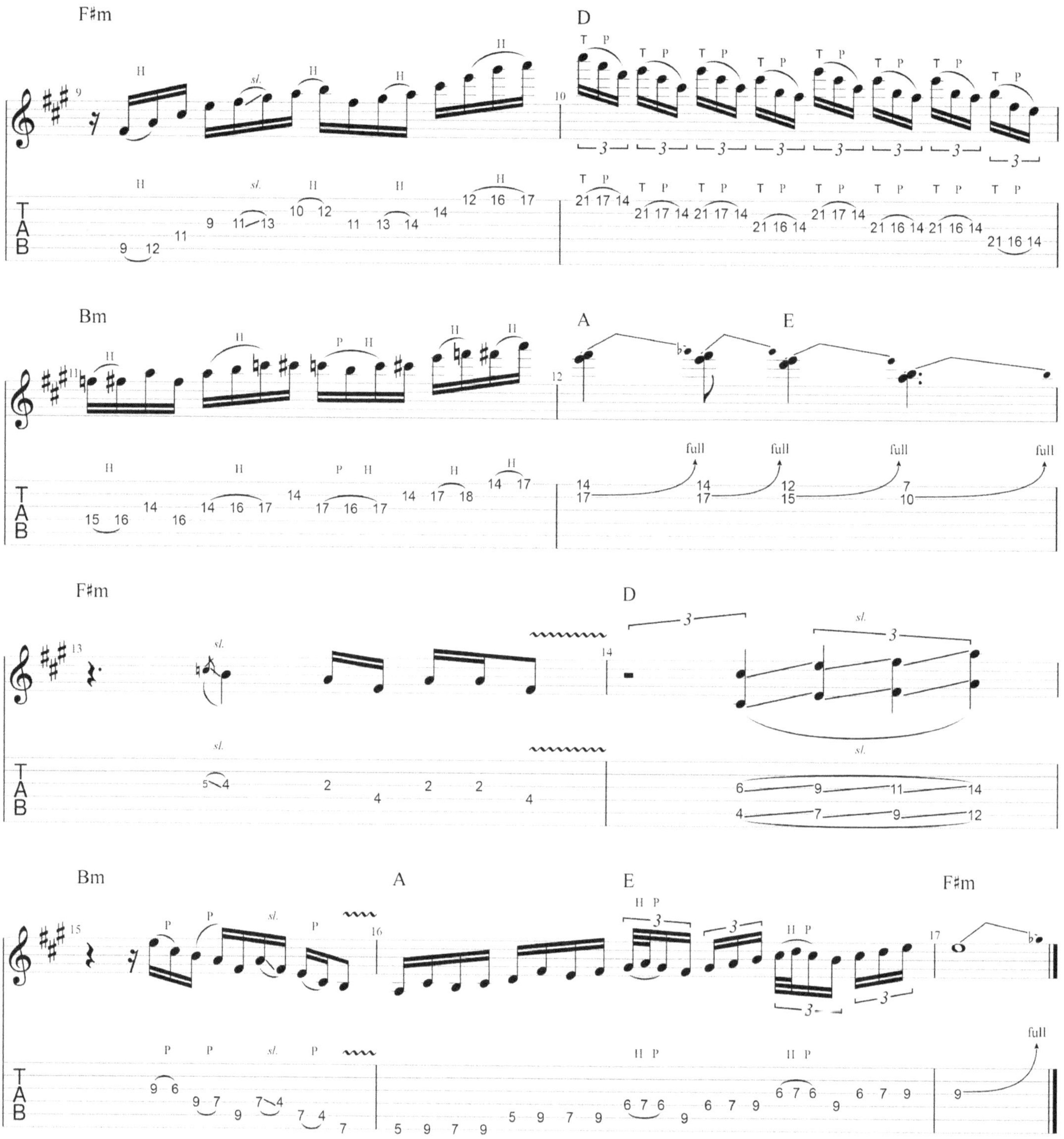
F♯m
D
Bm
A
E
F♯m
D
Bm
A
E
F♯m
full
sl.
TAB

A Gentleman's Conclusion

Congratulations! You've made it to the end of this book! Now you should have many approaches, sequences, licks and ideas to add to your improvised (and even composed) solos.

More important than just "doing what Chris said in his book" I have to stress the importance of finding *the thing* (or things) that make *your* playing personal and identifiable.

The journey of self-discovery is a long, harrowing and ever-changing one, and it is my hope that my learning, note choices and taste continues to evolve throughout my life. I wish all of my students and readers of this book to keep a similar, open mind. It all comes down to experimentation and finding your unique voice.

Keep shreddin', improving and composing those solos. Take some risks, get uncomfortable and discover some new and crazy ways to express yourself on the guitar.

Chris

Other Rock Guitar Books from Fundamental Changes

100 Classic Rock Licks for Guitar

Advanced Arpeggio Soloing for Guitar

Beyond Rhythm Guitar

Complete Technique for Modern Guitar

Exotic Pentatonic Soloing

Guitar – Pentatonic and Blues Scales

Guitar Fretboard Fluency

Heavy Metal Lead Guitar

Heavy Metal Rhythm Guitar

Melodic Rock Soloing for Guitar

Modern Music Theory for Guitarists

Neo-Classical Speed Strategies for Guitar

Progressive Metal Guitar

Rock Guitar Mode Mastery

Rock Guitar Un-CAGED

Rock Rhythm Guitar Playing

Slide Guitar Soloing Techniques

Sweep Picking Speed Strategies for Guitar

The Circle of Fifths for Guitarists

The Complete Technique Theory and Scales Compilation for Guitar

The Heavy Metal Guitar Bible

Ultimate Shred Machine

www.ingramcontent.com/pod-product-compliance
Lightning Source LLC
Chambersburg PA
CBHW081429090426
42740CB00017B/3236